D1569817

CODING CAREERS
IN THE ENERGY INDUSTRY

Jeri Freedman

Cavendish Square

New York

Published in 2020 by Cavendish Square Publishing, LLC
243 5th Avenue, Suite 136, New York, NY 10016

Library of Congress Cataloging-in-Publication Data

Names: Freedman, Jeri, author.
Title: Coding careers in the energy industry / Jeri Freedman.
Description: First edition. | New York : Cavendish Square, 2020. |
Series: Coding careers for tomorrow | Audience: Grades 7-12. |
Includes bibliographical references and index. | Identifiers: LCCN 2018057880 (print) |
LCCN 2018060853 (ebook) | ISBN 9781502645807 (ebook) | ISBN 9781502645791 (library bound) |
ISBN 9781502645784 (pbk.)Subjects: LCSH: Computer programming–Vocational guidance–
Juvenile literature. | Energy industries–Vocational guidance–Juvenile literature.
Classification: LCC QA76.6115 (ebook) | LCC QA76.6115 .F74 2020 (print) |
DDC 005.1023–dc23 LC record available at https://lccn.loc.gov/2018057880

Editorial Director: David McNamara
Editor: Kristen Susienka
Copy Editor: Denise Larrabee
Associate Art Director: Alan Sliwinski
Designer: Ginny Kemmerer
Production Coordinator: Karol Szymczuk
Photo Research: J8 Media

Printed in the United States of America

Contents

Large power plants, such as this one, generate and distribute energy.

chapter_01

The Energy Industry

Every aspect of modern life depends on energy—driving, traveling, and using electricity. Energy can be created in a variety of ways, but today all energy relies on computerization. Since computers require software code to operate, there are a great number of opportunities for coders in the energy industry.

GENERATING POWER

To generate power, one must convert a material or element (such as oil, gas, coal, wind, or sunlight) into another form. This process releases energy that can be used to power machinery or vehicles—or, in the case of electrical energy, distributed via wires to power electrical or electronic devices.

All energy generation and distribution systems begin with the locating and collecting of raw material (oil, coal, gas) or the building of apparatus to capture natural sources of energy (such as turbine waterwheels, windmills, or solar panels). Some power plants burn coal or natural gas to release heat energy, which they convert to electrical energy. Others convert the kinetic (motion) energy of water or wind to electrical energy, or do the same with heat energy from sunlight. Nuclear power plants use radiation from radioactive uranium to heat water. This produces steam, which is converted by a turbine into electricity.

Power plants distribute power in the form of electricity to homes and businesses by a system of wires, called the power grid. The companies that provide energy are called utilities. They must ensure that an adequate supply of power is provided to all buildings in the area they serve and that

Photovoltaic solar panels capture sunlight and convert it to electricity.

the power plants are operating safely as well as efficiently. Most of the steps in producing and distributing power and monitoring the operations of power plants are computerized. Among the common types of power generation systems are the following:

- Fossil fuel: These plants burn coal or natural gas. The heat is used to make steam, which is converted by a turbine generator into electric power. Some fuels such as coal and gasoline produce greenhouse gases as a by-product. These gases—carbon dioxide, for example—can harm the ozone layer, which protects Earth from damaging ultraviolet radiation from the sun. Natural gas, found in the ground, is clean-burning and does not produce such gases. Oil is primarily used to power home heating systems and is also processed into gasoline to run vehicles. When burned, oil and gasoline also produce greenhouse gases.

- Solar energy: Solar panels are used to collect sunlight. Solar panels that directly convert sunlight to electricity are called photovoltaic panels.

- Wind: Fields of windmills, called wind farms, capture kinetic energy from the motion of the wind. Solar panels and windmills do not produce harmful by-products.

- Hydroelectric: Hydroelectric systems use the kinetic energy of moving water. Modern hydroelectric plants use large dams. Water held on one side of the dam is released and flows over the blades of turbines connected to a generator, which transforms the mechanical energy into electric energy.

- Nuclear power: Nuclear energy relies on the splitting of atoms in rods of uranium (a process called fission) to be created. This process produces heat, which is used to make steam that is converted by a turbine generator into electricity. Because nuclear power plants do not burn fuel, they do not produce greenhouse gas emissions. However, if an accident were to occur, the radiation released could harm or kill people.

JOBS FOR CODERS IN THE ENERGY INDUSTRY

Traditionally, the energy-generation industry has relied heavily on mechanical operations overseen by human workers. In the twenty-first century, a technology revolution is altering the way that operations in the energy industry are carried out. Energy companies are developing and implementing software to streamline operations, improve production, and make distribution more efficient and cost-effective. They have begun to deploy smart grids, computerized control centers, wireless sensors for monitoring usage, predictive intelligence to prepare for changes in demand, and computer-based technologies that require programmers and coders. This transition in the energy industry has created a demand for programmers that is likely to continue to grow over the coming decades.

Coders are needed in the energy industry for a variety of applications. They write software to monitor remote sensors that track demand and

Wireless sensors on overhead power lines send data to a computer network via a device on the power pole.

automatically adjust the distribution of energy from a variety of sources. Software and sensors are also needed to monitor and provide information on the operation of equipment in order to avoid power outages and ensure the safety of workers and the general public. The increase in exploration of new areas of the country for oil drilling, such as the Bakken shale in the western United States, and the need for more power plants, mean that there is a steady demand for programs to analyze the impact of oil extraction and power plant construction on the environment. Programmers are especially needed in the areas of artificial intelligence (AI) and machine learning (ML), which are key aspects of power-generation automation and predictive technologies that allow companies to forecast future demand and prepare in advance to meet it.

EDITH CLARKE

Edith Clarke, the first female electrical engineer, worked on power system technology.

Edith Clarke was the first female electrical engineer in the United States. According to *Scientific American*, her innovative ideas can be considered the first steps toward smart grid technology. Clarke studied mathematics and astronomy at Vassar College, graduating in 1908. She went on to study civil engineering at Columbia University, and in 1918 she became the first woman to graduate from the Massachusetts Institute of Technology with a master's degree in electrical engineering. However, because she was a woman, she couldn't find work as an engineer. Therefore, she took a job as a supervisor of "computers," at General Electric (GE). Computers were employees, mostly women, who performed mathematical calculations. At GE, she invented the Clarke calculator in 1921. This was a tool that solved equations for calculating the electric current, voltage, and impedance along electric power lines. This information is necessary for power transmission. The Clarke calculator made it possible to perform such calculations ten times faster than previous methods.

In 1926, Clarke was the first woman to present a paper at the American Institute of Electrical Engineers' annual meeting. In 1947, she was hired by the University of Texas, where she taught for ten years, as the first female professor of electrical engineering in the United States. In 1948, Clarke became the first female Fellow of the American Institute of Electrical Engineers, and in 2015 she was inducted posthumously into the National Inventors Hall of Fame.

Electric lines on a transformer provide power to a region of India.

chapter_02

Coding's Impact on the Energy Industry

The production of energy is crucial to the functioning of every aspect of the economy. Seven billion people live on Earth, and producing adequate energy to meet their needs is a massive undertaking. Methods of generating and distributing energy have changed over time and continue to evolve. As people have become more aware of the effects that burning fossil fuels can have on the environment, these concerns have come to play a bigger role in how energy is generated. By 2040, the population of the world is projected to grow close to nine billion people. This increase in population, and improvements in the standard of living of people in developing nations, will create a much larger demand for energy. However, that demand must be met while addressing issues of climate change, to which energy generation contributes.

A BRIEF HISTORY OF THE ENERGY INDUSTRY

Since earliest times, harnessing energy has been the key to advancing civilization and improving people's lives. Basic machines run by steam were present as far back as ancient Egypt. This was merely the beginning of energy production. As populations expanded and people sought ways to travel and trade with one another, old forms of energy were improved and new technologies were invented.

EARLY POWER GENERATION

Over time, steam engine technology continually improved. In the mid-1700s, Thomas Newcomen and James Watt introduced adaptations into the design of steam engines, producing the first modern steam engine. Modern steam-powered engines made the Industrial Revolution of the nineteenth and twentieth centuries possible, allowing for automated production in factories. By the 1800s, steam engines powered farm equipment, trains and ships, and factory machinery. In 1880, Thomas Edison revolutionized the power industry when he attached a coal-powered steam

This illustration shows nineteenth-century factory workers checking spools of cotton automatically spun by steam-powered machinery.

engine to the first electric generator at his plant in New York City. The electricity generated powered the first electric lights for Wall Street and the *New York Times*.

In 1882, the first hydroelectric electricity-generating plant in the world went into operation in Appleton, Wisconsin. By the late 1800s, automobiles began to hit the roads. Initially there were competing steam-, electric-, and gasoline-powered versions of cars. The internal combustion engine, which burned gasoline to power the car, won out, so the processing of oil into gasoline, to feed internal combustion engines, became an industry. By 1908, Henry Ford had perfected the process of mass-producing cars on an assembly

In the late 1800s, electric streetlights began to appear in New York City. This illustration shows some on Wall Street during that time.

line, and automobiles became affordable for the middle class. From the early 1900s to the present, energy needs have steadily increased. The growing industrialization of developing nations, world population growth, and an ever-increasing number of electric—and later electronic—devices have fueled this increase in demand. Throughout the 1900s, energy demand doubled every ten years. Power plants grew in size, resulting in huge hydroelectric dams and coal-fired plants. The network of transmission lines, substations, transformers, and other components that distribute energy from the plant to homes and businesses is referred to as the electrical grid, or just "the grid."

THE TWENTIETH CENTURY AND BEYOND

The ability to use nuclear power to produce energy was developed—along with the atom bomb—during World War II. After the end of the war in 1945, the US government looked to nuclear energy as a way to produce large amounts of electricity. They built power plants that provided energy to customers in nearby towns and cities. However, accidents such as the partial meltdown of the Three Mile Island nuclear power plant near Middletown, Pennsylvania, in 1979 inhibited public acceptance of nuclear power, and very few new plants were built in the United States. Nuclear energy–based power

The Three Mile Island nuclear power plant was the site of one of the worst nuclear power accidents in history.

plants are more common in some other parts of the world, such as Europe, especially in areas where fossil fuels are not easily available.

In the late twentieth century and early twenty-first century, concerns about pollution from burning fossil fuels led to a search for alternate forms of energy that were "cleaner." Coal production decreased from its peak in 2008 to 2016, and then increased slightly by about 6 percent in 2017. Although the Trump administration removed some environmental regulations on coal plants in 2017, this mainly eased expenses only on existing plants, and as of 2018 there are no plans to build more coal-fired plants. Instead, the energy industry is continuing to build renewable resources, such as wind farms, and to burn natural gas, which is cheap and abundant in the United States, where it is often found along with petroleum. Natural gas does not produce the same by-products as coal, so it is a cleaner, or more environmentally friendly, source of energy. Renewable energy production and consumption has also continued to grow. In 2017, production and consumption achieved record highs of about eleven quadrillion British thermal units (Btu). Btu is a standard measure of energy output based on how much heat is required to raise 1 pound of water by 1 degree Fahrenheit. The growth in renewable energy production and consumption was mostly from increased solar and wind resources. Hydroelectric power production remained stable.

CODING IN THE ENERGY INDUSTRY

The oil, gas, and electricity industries are eager to adopt and apply new techniques that improve efficiency and profitability. Many companies are just beginning the process of digitization, which provides many opportunities for coders. In some instances, the terms "programmer" and "coder" are used interchangeably to mean "a person who provides software that allows a computer to perform a particular function." In other cases, the term "programmer" is used to mean "a person who creates an original software program," and the term "coder" is used to refer to "a person who uses existing software to create an application to perform a specific task." For example, data mining is the process of collecting and analyzing large amounts of data. A coder might use data-mining software to create a unique application that looks for patterns of energy usage among a particular company's customers. As more software has become available that can be used to create customized applications, the demand for coders is growing at a faster rate than the demand for programmers to create original software.

The "cloud" consists of remote computers that provide space for data to individual companies. Some cloud providers are independent companies, but large organizations, such as utilities, often contract for cloud space and services with large corporations such as IBM, Apple, Google, or Microsoft because these companies offer very large data capacity.

A Smarter Grid

According to the US Department of Energy (DOE), the grid "consists of more than 9,200 electric generating units with more than 1 million megawatts of generating capacity connected to more than 300,000 miles [over 482,800 kilometers] of transmission lines." The grid was built in the 1890s and has grown in a haphazard fashion over the

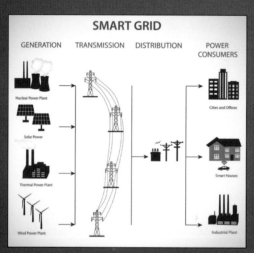

decades. To meet modern demand, it needs to be rebuilt in a way that incorporates digital technology, and automated to meet the complex needs of the twenty-first century and beyond. The US Department of Energy is spearheading the

This graphic shows how electricity will be generated and distributed via the smart grid.

effort to create the smart grid. It will use computers, automation, and software to make a system that automatically distributes energy from various sources to where it is needed, changing its distribution as demand ebbs and flows. The smart grid will reduce the occurrence of brownouts and blackouts, periods of time when sections of the grid fail in certain areas and plunge these areas into darkness, and better equip the electrical systems to respond to emergencies, including both natural disasters and man-made catastrophes. Because components of the system will communicate automatically, the system will be able to detect power outages immediately and reroute resources to those areas. It will schedule teams to repair damages faster and help maintain emergency power for health centers, police and fire departments, traffic lights, and the phone system. Coders and programmers will be required at all levels to implement the software for all of the system's components.

In many cases, they also provide tools for clients to create applications, as well as consultants to help implement them. A coder in the energy industry might work with the team at such a cloud provider.

The availability of affordable large-scale computing power is enabling greater and more widespread exploration for oil and gas, and more automation of power generation and distribution systems. In addition, energy management and control systems (EMACS) allow better integration of planning, control, and monitoring of power distribution, and make it easier to balance and shift power from low-demand to high-demand areas in real time.

Energy companies are making large investments in digitized hardware and software for power plants, substations, and transmission and distribution networks. Coders create applications that ultimately form systems that have fewer disruptions, maintain higher loads, and last longer, which reduces costs and improves efficiency. Therefore, utilities have come to see information technology as a vital tool for their transmission and distribution networks.

Among the applications needed by utilities are those for the following tasks:

- **Managing the flow of power**

- **Analyzing disruptions in the power supply after they occur**

- Analyzing historical data—both power distribution data and customer-related data

- Analyzing power generator performance

- Providing financial and operational analysis

Increasingly, energy companies are implementing operational information systems (OISs). OISs provide data on business activities, such as financial, sales, and purchasing transactions. These systems are separate from those used to run the power generation and distribution side of their businesses. This is a relatively new area and provides new opportunities for programmers and coders. Applications are required to analyze the vast quantity of data that exists in companies' operational and financial databases. Coders must convert this information into easily understood reports, charts, and graphs that illustrate the findings.

MANAGING UTILITY CUSTOMERS

People in many areas have access to a variety of energy suppliers. They can choose which company provides their oil, natural gas, and electricity services. Therefore, if energy companies are to succeed, it is important for them to attract and retain as many customers as possible. Beginning in the late 1990s, companies in the energy industry began to employ customer information systems (CISs) designed specifically for utilities. Initially, such systems focused mostly on the practical

JOBS LOST and GaineD

As automation and digitization advance in the energy industry, the number of workers for some traditional hands-on jobs will be reduced. Smart meters that can be read remotely from a truck that is driven past a house or business are already being implemented in some areas. Such technology reduces the number of workers who read meters manually. As part of the smart grid, meters will simply send their monthly data automatically to customer billing systems, without any need for meter readers. More billing operations will likely occur automatically as well, as a result of information transmitted directly into the system. Automated call centers and self-service customer portals reduce the need for human workers too. Service scheduling may also become an automated process.

At the same time that advances in technology are replacing some jobs, they are creating new ones. The majority of these jobs will be technical: engineers, computer programmers, and coders. Programmers and coders will be needed to write the software and applications that run in-house digitized systems at energy-related companies and utilities, upgrade them as needed, and analyze the data produced by them. They will also be needed to create, test, and upgrade the software used for the smart grid—a process that will take many years. For those presently in high school, this is an excellent time to become a coder in the energy industry, as demand for coders is likely to be high for quite some time.

aspects of customer management, relating primarily to the financial aspects of the business, such as maintaining account records, processing orders, billing customers, and collecting payments. They were also used for service call management. These systems often required individual software programs and were not well integrated. They provided little insight into the nature of the company's customers.

Utilities now want to improve their relationships with customers, to better attract and retain them. They want to be able to respond to changes in the demand for energy created by the proliferation of electronic devices and electric cars. They want to be able to bring new products to market faster, and to reduce services costs as well. To address these needs, companies in the energy industry are adopting flexible computer systems and software that can be expanded as the volume of data increases. Companies are integrating systems—combining information from the business and the power generation parts of the business to provide insights into customers' and power demand requirements.

Implementing applications for such customer information systems requires coders. These applications include the following:

- **Providing information for the call center marketing system to better manage consumer and business-to-business sales campaigns.**

- Supporting business planning by using data mining to predict customers' near-term future needs and interests.

- Improving business management by providing better workflow control and electronic data interchange (EDI) among computer systems. In EDI, one computer system is able to automatically download data to a different computer system, such as a financial billing system automatically sending data to a customer service call center system. Such systems can also provide information on employees to human resources departments to help companies better retain workers. In addition, they support billing and debt management operations.

- Providing operations management applications, including insight into risks for better risk management, and management of suppliers and partners.

Utility companies, like many companies in numerous other industries, are moving to online self-service systems for customer service. These systems offer advantages for both customers and the company. Customers have the convenience of being able to access their accounts, pay bills, check for power outages in their area, report problems, and schedule service appointments online at any time, not merely when the company's customer service department is open. Many such self-service systems are integrated with automated call center systems, which allow customers to call in and access a variety of service options by phone, using voice recognition applications. Even when a customer is transferred to a live person to complete a transaction, computerization of the call center is useful. If the automated system is integrated with the company's database, scheduling, and billing systems, it can provide the human representative with necessary information about the customer, and that allows issues to be dealt with faster. Companies benefit when customers can handle transactions without interacting with a live person, which reduces costs. Creating such systems and integrating them with the company's other computer and database systems requires coders for both the software itself and the website through which the customer interacts with the system. Digitization is playing a key role in the energy industry. However, many companies are just starting to implement sensor-based monitoring and control systems and customer relationship management systems. Market research firm KPMG's "US CEO Outlook 2017" survey revealed that 72 percent of chief executive officers (CEOs) feel that it is important to implement digital technologies to stay current with or ahead of their competitors. This finding applies to the deregulated energy market, where power companies face competition for customers. According to the KPMG survey, 45 percent

A smart meter like this one automatically sends energy usage data to a utility company.

of CEOs believe they are not using digital technologies effectively. Coders are not just needed to implement digital programs for energy production, distribution, and customer management systems. They are also needed to ensure the security of the data acquisition and management programs.

They must implement cybersecurity programs to ensure that the power distribution systems and company databases are safe from hackers, who could cause power disruptions or steal vital customer or company information.

The implementation of digital technologies is going to result in the interconnection of energy systems throughout the world. Energy systems will become smarter, more efficient and reliable, and sustainable. Coders will play a major role in implementing the technologies that make these advances possible.

A blackout shuts down operations at businesses and inconveniences consumers in New York City in 2012.

chapter_03

New Technologies in the Energy Industry

Computer-controlled equipment, monitoring, and analysis play a key role in reliably providing electricity. These technologies are used in power plants, homes, and businesses to monitor and control energy-producing and -distributing equipment. Interruptions in the availability of power can cost the economy several billion dollars every year. However, making sure that interruptions don't occur in the power supply is a difficult task. Consumers as well as companies are looking for ways to reduce their energy costs. Automated monitoring technology can help. New artificial intelligence, machine learning, and deep learning computer technologies will provide benefits for the energy industry and consumers.

TECHNOLOGY FOR BETTER ENERGY

The failure of a single component among thousands used in a plant can result in a shutdown. The utility responsible for this type of problem loses income since customers can't use electricity, and it might lead to losing customers. More important, since many people rely on power to operate daily tasks, a power shutdown affects customers' ability to perform these activities. To reduce drops in power, many

A power line repair crew replaces an old electrical transformer.

plants are interconnected. Together, they form regional transmission systems. Such systems allow electricity to be diverted from areas of low usage to those with more demand at any given time. However, these systems are complex and sometimes require generators thousands of miles apart to be synchronized.

Software programmers must design programs that run such networks. The use of software and sensors to monitor parts and equipment is necessary to improve the reliability of the electric power supply and provide cost-effective maintenance. A sensor is a device that monitors the state of a system component and sends data about its status to a computer. For example, a temperature sensor in an automobile monitors the temperature of the engine. It sends information to the car's computer, and if the temperature gets too high, it might alert the driver with a light on the dashboard. Sensors can detect places where a power failure is likely to occur and provide advance warning, improving the safety and reliability of the system.

The biggest change in the way that power is distributed is the use of artificial intelligence and machine learning in the power system. Artificial intelligence is the use of software to simulate human intelligence in order to make complex decisions in a way that mimics human logic. Machine learning is the process by which computers improve their analytical and decision-making processes based on experience—much in the way that human beings learn. In machine learning, computers use a series of rules, called algorithms, to analyze vast volumes of data, detect patterns in it, and provide decisions or predictions according to patterns it finds. In machine learning software, the results of various decisions are analyzed by the computer software to identify the best choices.

Deep learning is an advanced form of machine learning. It uses a technique called neural networks in combination with massive sets of data to allow a program to train itself. Neural network systems consist of a collection of connected units, called nodes, often referred to as artificial neurons. The collection of artificial neurons mimics the neurons that make up the human brain. Neural networks are not programmed by given rules. Instead, they are set a goal and use trial and error to create possible ways to reach the goal. These solutions are ranked, and the best are kept. Then the analysis is run again, and the selection of the best solutions occurs again. This process continues with the computer "learning" more with each analysis.

AI and ML are necessary to analyze vast quantities of data to find meaningful patterns, because human beings cannot quickly sort through such large quantities of data manually. Programming artificial intelligence and machine learning systems is a major area with demand for coders. AI and ML allow a complex system, which includes remote sensors, various traditional and alternative sources of energy, and the smart grid, to monitor and adjust itself to predict upcoming energy and maintenance needs, respond to demand, and ensure safety, with minimal human intervention.

Huge amounts of data, called big data, is now available. The data is created on or captured from computer systems and sensors. AI and ML can be used to analyze big data because computers with multiple processors are now capable of providing massive computational power at low cost, and drives capable of storing very large amounts of data have become less expensive. These factors make it possible to analyze huge amounts of data cost effectively. Using such large varied data sets makes machine learning more accurate.

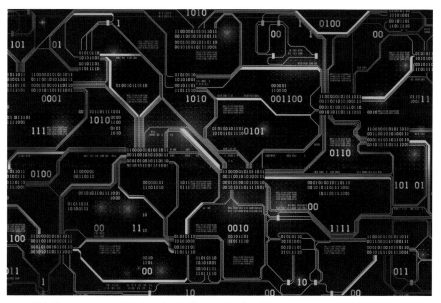

This is a concept of a futuristic electronic circuit board that uses a neural network.

An energy management system is used to control energy usage throughout a facility.

Companies such as Google, Microsoft, Amazon, and IBM have set up services to help companies such as utilities apply these new technologies, which makes their implementation more attractive. Many operations in the energy industry are just starting to venture into applying these technologies, so there is plenty of opportunity for coders and programmers to get involved.

SMARTER ENERGY USAGE

Utilities are not the only companies within the energy industry in which coders are needed. Private businesses also employ coders to help big industrial companies improve energy usage. One such company is Verdigris Technologies, located in Mountain View, California. The company, founded in 2011, provides an artificial intelligence–based system to help clients manage their energy usage. The system is used to control energy consumption in large commercial buildings and business facilities.

In this approach, smart sensors are attached to a company's electrical circuits, providing the ability to track energy consumption. The sensors send the collected data to Verdigris via wireless computer technology. Information is processed at Verdigris, and the client company is able to check a dashboard on its computers 24/7. Computer software allows Verdigris to monitor each individual appliance or machine. For example, the company has successfully identified preventable inefficiencies in energy usage for the San Francisco–based W Hotel.

Another company, PowerScout, applies AI-based software to energy industry data to predict ways that energy costs can possibly be reduced. PowerScout suggests ways that consumers can make changes in their homes to improve their energy usage and reduce costs. The company helps clients form decisions regarding renewable energy purchases for their homes.

These are merely two companies using software to address the energy needs of businesses and consumers. There is likely to be a growing number of companies using data mining and AI to provide energy-related analysis and advisory services in the future. These companies will require programmers to create both programs to collect and analyze data, and software to monitor and report on energy consumption and provide client recommendations.

APPLICATIONS FOR AI IN THE ENERGY INDUSTRY

The following are some applications for AI in the energy industry. Load forecasting is the prediction of how much energy is going to be needed in a given location. Predicting how much energy will be needed in the short term is key to making sure it is available to meet spikes in demand and avoid shortages. It also allows utilities to reduce the amount of fuel used to produce energy when it is likely that demand is going to be low. The more efficient use of fuel helps control the company's costs. Since these costs are passed on to consumers in the form of higher charges, it also helps customers keep their energy costs down. In a process known as yield optimization, software is used to monitor devices such as windmills on wind farms and optimize the turbine on each windmill as it runs. This process allows them to generate more energy.

Software is needed for predictive maintenance. This process uses patterns identified by AI to signal when maintenance is likely to be required on a component. Software is also needed to program drones that can be used to inspect

A robotic energy system inspection drone checks power distribution components at a power plant in China.

components such as power lines. Deep learning algorithms created by programmers can be used to train drones to find defects and predict failures. In addition to being safer and less time-consuming than manual inspections, inspections by drones can be done without interrupting operations.

Artificial Intelligence for Renewable Energy

Renewable energy sources are those that regenerate naturally as they are used, such as wind or solar energy. Such sources produce less pollution than fossil fuels and don't consume natural resources. However, there are issues related to operating renewable energy sources, including predicting how weather will affect them, in order to maximize the production of energy and improve efficiency. Companies are hiring programmers to explore the application of artificial intelligence to renewable energy. A major challenge of renewable energy sources is that the energy they produce fluctuates with changes in the weather. Artificial intelligence–based computer programs can assist with the forecasting of weather, using detailed reports from weather stations and satellite data. This data will be used to provide more accurate predictions of how much power will be generated by renewable energy sources such as wind farms. Knowing days in advance the quantity of energy that will be available from renewable sources will allow companies to more accurately plan for how much energy will need to be produced from traditional sources, leading to more efficient use of equipment and fossil fuels. This helps reduce pollution and costs.

AI and ML can be used to automate a system's response to demand for energy in real time. With this technology, the utility draws on energy provided by traditional and alternative energy sources to meet demand as it increases and decreases in specific parts of its coverage area. Using this method, computer programs continually estimate the flow of energy from various resources.

In the oil and gas industries, artificial intelligence–based computer programs can help solve a range of problems, from locating potential sources of oil and gas to monitoring operations. Artificial intelligence–based computer systems can be used both to predict where a component or line is likely to fail and to recommend the type of corrective action most likely to succeed. Oil and gas companies need to minimize their costs and reduce their risks in order to survive. Data mining and artificial intelligence–based computer programs can be used to improve performance in both these areas.

Artificial intelligence can also be applied to the business side of the energy industry. Companies need programmers to develop programs that monitor customers' behavior and respond to their queries. Artificial intelligence–based computer programs can be used to analyze customers' energy usage patterns and flag unusual variations that might indicate a problem. AI can also be used to increase utilities' income by providing insight into customers' behavior and potential requirements. Companies can use this information to create individual offers for additional products or services targeted at customers who might need them. In many locations, customers can choose from various suppliers for their oil, electricity, and natural gas. Developing relationships with customers in this way can help companies keep customers and increase their revenues.

Programmers are needed to create programs that automate the process of responding to customers' queries in call centers. The creation of virtual agents allows computerized responses to customers' questions and provides instant assistance. From the accounting side, computer programs are used to monitor customers' payment history and alert personnel to customers who are unlikely to pay their bill.

Artificial intelligence–based systems use data obtained from households with smart meters—meters that send energy usage data back to the utility. Data from these customers can be analyzed to identify which appliances are using specific amounts of energy and how much of a customer's energy bill is attributable to each type of usage. This type of service allows customers to reduce their costs by upgrading energy-hungry appliances or changing their pattern of usage. Using AI and ML to analyze this type of data from a large number of users allows companies to provide such information even to homes that don't have smart meters.

Computer programs that incorporate analytical, predictive, and AI and ML technologies are being integrated into the existing energy infrastructure, and this offers an exciting range of possibilities for improving energy distribution and customer relationships. However, adoption of such technologies is just beginning in the energy sector. This means that there are many opportunities for coders, and the demand is likely to increase, making this a fruitful area in which to look for work.

A data analyst creates a graph to illustrate relationships among data.

chapter_04

Coding Jobs in the Energy Field

In the energy industry, jobs for coders and programmers include research and analysis interns, and junior and senior analysts and programmers. These professionals work for large and small organizations, and for government agencies, in both traditional and alternative energy. Coders will find employment not only at utilities but also in contract software development companies, and in government agencies such as the US Department of Energy.

DATA AND OPERATIONS ANALYSTS

Data and operational analysts use their knowledge of math, science, and engineering to create and apply computer-based analysis to extract and interpret information from data collected and stored in company databases. They work with advanced software to aid energy companies with forecasting and predicting energy requirements. The information they supply assists utilities in decision-making and improving energy generation and distribution efficiency.

Most data analysts have a bachelor's degree, although an associate's degree or professional certification plus work experience can be acceptable for some entry-level jobs. Being an operations research analyst usually requires a bachelor's degree, and many employers prefer candidates with a master's degree. Operational analysts need to take a combination of mathematics and statistics courses, as well as computer science. Some candidates have dual degrees in operations research and computer science, which make them particularly desirable to employers.

Junior analysts serve as part of a team, learning the different activities involved in the energy business. They are supervised by a senior analyst. They might also participate in company-sponsored workshops designed to enhance their skills. Senior analysts perform high-level data analytics tasks and manage project teams. They evaluate the requirements for an analysis project, estimate the resources and time required to create the code and complete the project, and track the project's progress and costs. Senior analyst positions usually require a college degree and several years of coding experience, preferably in the energy industry.

A senior analyst supervises a junior analyst working on a software application.

RESEARCH ANALYSTS

Research analysts create and maintain databases that contain information used to answer research questions being investigated by the operations or research personnel at energy companies or federal or state energy research laboratories. Research analysts use software to create queries that pull information from the data collected and housed in databases. They perform computer-based analyses on the data and format it into tables and charts. This position requires at least a bachelor's degree in computer science or a related area. Higher-level positions might require a master's degree. Research analysts must be familiar with the software used in the energy operations field, such as the computer language Python and specialized utility software. Research laboratory software will include applications such as LabVIEW and MATLAB, which are used to analyze measurements taken in the field, as well as Python.

SOFTWARE DEVELOPERS/ PROGRAMMERS

Software developers, or programmers, create, test, and implement the applications that run on computers. The computer systems that control the energy generation, distribution, and analysis processes need industry-specific software. Software developers also modify existing computer programs to adapt them to specific utility and company needs. In addition, they integrate software applications from a variety of systems so that data can be shared. Programmers often work on teams with a lead or senior programmer as the head of the team. Therefore, programming jobs are available from entry level to senior level. Entry-level software programmers might only have job experience and a certificate showing they have mastered particular software languages used in the industry, or an associate's degree. Most have a bachelor's degree, and some of those in higher-level positions have a master's degree. The most important element for gaining a programming job is hands-on experience.

APPLICATIONS PROGRAMMERS

Applications programmers create and modify computer application software or specialized utility programs. They work with users and managers to identify their requirements and then develop programs to meet those needs. They often work with other members of a programming team. They might provide solutions for partner companies or suppliers, as well as the company they work for. They create guides for personnel on how to use the software they develop, as well as document the processes they used to develop the programs, in case they need to be modified in the future. This job requires knowledge of popular applications software, such as SQL and Oracle, and familiarity with programming languages used in the energy and business field, including Python. Because applications are often developed for use by personnel working beyond the company's premises—such as those collecting data at wind farms or solar array sites— experience with software used to create smartphone and web applications might be required.

BIG DATA PROGRAMMER

Big data programmers develop programs to process very large quantities of data, such as that collected in large databases and by smart grid remote sensors. These programmers create and modify software to find answers to complex operational and business problems. This position requires

GEOGRAPHICAL INFORMATION SYSTEMS PROGRAMMER/ANALYST

Geographic information systems programmers work on a mapping application.

A geographic information system (GIS) is a system designed to capture, store, manipulate, analyze, manage, and present all types of geographical data. Geographical information systems provide visual information about the nature of the terrain in an area. They show the location and density of particular features, both man-made (such as mines) and natural (such as oil-producing shale). They can also show the density of a population in a given area. In addition, they can project changes that might be produced in an area by mining, oil drilling, or construction of a hydroelectric dam or power plant.

GIS programmers and analysts in the energy industry develop geospatial software and tools to capture data about the terrain and features of a physical area. They analyze the data and format information to be displayed in the form of a map. They create GIS applications to analyze terrain for mining and oil companies and utilities. They might analyze land-based and aerial imagery, as well as data in databases, to produce specialized maps. They interpret data, identify trends, and note patterns in data. Most GIS programmers have at least a bachelor's degree. It is also possible to obtain certification through professional organizations, such as the Urban and Regional Information Systems Association (URISA) and the American Society of Photogrammetry and Remote Sensing (ASPRS), or GIS software companies, such as Esri. Certification is not mandatory, but it can be beneficial when seeking a job.

This futuristic image illustrates a programmer creating advanced software to analyze very large quantities of data.

knowledge of how to create software to collect and analyze vast quantities of data and to manage large-scale databases and data warehouses. Big data programmers also need to know artificial intelligence and machine learning techniques, and must understand particular software, such as Kafka, that is used for big data analysis. They must be familiar with both big data systems (such as Hadoop, Cassandra, MongoDB, and Redshift) and traditional database software (such as Oracle, SQL, and SAP). Candidates also need experience using statistical analysis tools and languages used to create machine learning software, such as R, SAS, and Python. In addition to technical skills, big data programmers must have good people skills to work with business and partner company personnel to create the models that help guide technology decisions.

INTERNSHIPS

Internships allow students to work with industry professionals and learn firsthand what it is like to be a coder in the energy field. Internships are usually unpaid or low-paid positions that students undertake to gain hands-on experience and learn the ropes in the real world. Some internships are arranged as part of a computer science or engineering program at a university. Others are advertised on job search, energy industry organization, or individual company websites. Internship opportunities exist in government agencies,

A programmer instructs an intern in the use of energy-industry software.

research organizations, and private companies and utilities. Interns usually perform basic tasks to assist researchers or software developers in an organization. They might write the documentation and assist with the implementation, testing, deployment, and maintenance of existing and new software applications.

Both the US Department of Energy and many state departments of energy offer internships for students studying coding. The DOE provides paid internships for students enrolled in a high school, or at least part-time in a technical, vocational, or two- or four-year college. It provides two types of paid internships: the Student Temporary Employment Program (STEP) and the Student Career Experience Program (SCEP). In STEP, the student works in a position that is not necessarily related to coding but provides the opportunity to learn about the nature and issues of the energy industry. In SCEP, a student works in an area directly related to their academic or career area of interest—in this case, coding.

The DOE also offers the Mickey Leland Energy Fellowship at locations around the United States. Named after the late George Thomas "Mickey" Leland, antipoverty activist and congressman, this is a ten-week summer internship program specifically for women and minority college students whose academic major is in science, technology, engineering, or math. More information about these programs can be found on the DOE student internship web page (https://www.energy.gov/student-programs-and-internships).

In addition to the federal government, many state departments of energy fund research facilities investigating research areas such as renewable energy. They offer internships that give students a chance to practice coding skills in the energy field by assisting in computer modeling, programming, or collecting and analyzing data. For example, the Alaska Center for Energy and Power employs interns to assist researchers in renewable energy with analyzing data related to energy use and consumption. To find internship opportunities in a particular state, one can contact the state's department of energy or national laboratory, or visit its website.

Private companies in the energy field also hire interns in programming and data science. Companies offering internships include renewable energy providers operating wind farms and solar panel arrays, oil and gas companies, mining companies, software companies that create software for the energy industry, and utilities. An example of the types of work performed by an intern is provided by a six-month internship at Dominion Energy, a West Virginia utility, for a college student intending to major in computer science. The intern would work as part of a software team that builds, deploys, and maintains applications for internal customers.

Internships not only allow students to develop coding skills related to the energy field, but also give them the opportunity to experience a job firsthand and decide whether coding and the energy industry are right for them. Undertaking multiple internships over the course of one's education can help one decide which area of coding in the energy industry one prefers. In addition, internships allow students to develop relationships with professionals in the industry. These contacts can be valuable for referrals or references when later seeking a job. An internship also provides one with experience that can be included on a résumé when job hunting, and demonstrates to potential employers that one is capable of performing the tasks required of an entry-level analyst or programmer.

CHALLENGES AND ADVANTAGES

Advantages of a coding job in the energy industry include the option of working for a large or small company. Large companies offer higher pay and many benefits. In addition, large companies often provide great job security. Sometimes they will pay for college courses taken in a field related to an employee's job. This is an excellent way for a coder in an entry-level job to pursue advanced education while working.

In a small or alternative energy company, one can often work in a more flexible and entrepreneurial environment, and have the opportunity to help build a business and improve the environment. As the worldwide demand for energy increases, and automation and data analytics play an ever-larger role in energy generation, distribution, and sales, the demand for coders is going to remain high. Pay in the field is good, and there is a steady career path from entry-level to mid-level to senior-level positions, with increasing pay and responsibility. The disadvantages of any coding career include having to work long hours when information or a program is needed by a deadline. Coding projects in the energy industry are performed by teams, so one might have to deal with difficult coworkers and make compromises. Also, coders may have to travel to substations within a company's distribution area, and in the case of multistate and multinational companies, travel may be substantial.

Students studying for a college degree do hands-on projects in a computer lab.

chapter_05

Learning to Be a Programmer

Programmers need both technical and personal skills. To obtain a coding job in the energy field, you will need to know the computer languages used in that industry, such as Python, as well as general software used to create database, data-mining, and business applications. There is no way to know exactly what type of coding you will do on the job. You might have to create software that analyzes data from sensors, or a mobile app for the company's customers. You might work with data-mining applications that look for patterns in data stored in databases or acquired in real time from sensors in the field. Therefore, it is important to develop the basic skills that can allow you to learn various languages, applications, and statistical techniques.

PREPARING IN HIGH SCHOOL

Coders in the energy industry will often work on programs designed to monitor power lines and the equipment that generates and distributes power. Therefore, they need to understand the principles of math and physics that govern the operation of equipment and the generation of electricity. They also need to understand the mathematics required to create computer algorithms. Consequently, studying math and physics in high school is necessary for a solid foundation for further education in this field. For those who plan to go into fields related to oil and gas, courses in chemistry and geology are also useful. Since energy production and distribution have significant effects on the environment, courses in earth science or ecology can be helpful, especially for those interested in working with alternative energy and energy research.

Computer algorithms rely on a branch of mathematics called calculus. To prepare for courses in calculus and other advanced mathematics courses in college, you should take classes in algebra and precalculus in high school. (If your school offers a course in calculus, you should take that as well.) It is also important to understand statistics. The mathematical methods taught in a statistics course are used to analyze data for both operational and business purposes.

On the job, you will need to communicate effectively, both verbally and in writing. You will, at some point in your career, have to make presentations to management, customers, and partner companies. You will create reports about the results of your analysis. You will share information with other programmers, in-house managers, and staff. This means you must learn to organize your ideas and speak and write in a way that is clear—especially to people who do not have knowledge of programming or data analysis. You need to have a solid understanding of English grammar and syntax. Using proper grammar and syntax makes your meaning clear. In addition, doing so makes you sound more professional, which makes your listeners more likely to respect your opinion.

Doing presentations in high school provides practice in speaking to large groups of people.

If your school offers a course in public speaking, taking it can help you hone your communications skills. Coders spend most of their time at a keyboard. You will be more efficient if you develop fast typing or keyboarding skills.

DEVELOPING YOUR CODING SKILLS

One excellent way to prepare for a software development career is to gain experience while you are still in high school. In some schools it is possible to take courses in computers or join computer clubs in which students practice creating software programs. If your school offers such an option, take advantage of it. Trying out coding is the best way to see if a career as a programmer will interest you. Practicing coding gives you firsthand knowledge of the types of problems you will encounter in the real world and how to solve them. You can practice creating apps yourself. Companies such as Apple and Microsoft offer development kits for those interested in making apps. You can share apps with friends, post about them on a social media site such as Twitter, or even offer them through a site that sells apps, such as Apple's App Store or Google's Play Store. Making your own app can be satisfying, but it also requires patience and hours of work. There are many ways to gain computing and programming skills, including courses, books, and CDs that offer training in specific languages such as Python.

Another way to gain knowledge is to join a professional organization. There are both computing industry organizations and energy industry organizations that can help in your development. Two of the largest computing industry organizations are the Association for Computing Machinery (ACM) and the Institute of Electrical and Electronics Engineers (IEEE). These organizations provide standards and information related to computing for the energy industry and others. Among the major energy industry organizations are the American Solar Energy Society (ASES), the Association of Energy Engineers (AEE), and the Society of Petroleum Engineers (SPE). All these organizations have student memberships and special resources for students.

EDUCATION FOR CODING

Most programming jobs require a four-year college degree. In some cases, experienced programmers are hired without one, but the environment is competitive for those just starting out. For some junior positions, an associate's degree in programming might be acceptable, especially if combined with on-the-job experience from part-time, summer, or internship jobs. Many colleges offer four-year bachelor's degrees as well as master's and PhD degrees in these fields. Technical institutes offer both four-year degree programs and two-year associate's degree programs. It is also possible to

WIND POWER DATA ANALYST

A wind farm data analyst analyzes measured wind data and produces energy estimates for companies that manage wind farms. He or she analyzes the performance of existing wind farms and provides estimates of power generation for projects being developed. The analyst spends the bulk of his or her time working on a computer, using wind assessment software and models. He or she also visits project sites and attends meetings and conferences. To obtain this type of job, the candidate must have at least a bachelor's degree in computer science or a degree that combines computer science with engineering, meteorology, or mathematics. He or she must have learned to use the software required for the job, such as MATLAB, Microsoft Word, Microsoft Excel, and GIS, either in school, through separate courses, or on a previous

Wind power data analysts capture data from the windmills in a wind farm.

job. In addition, the analyst must have developed the skills to work well with other team members and be creative in dealing with technical issues and solving problems. He or she must have developed strong communication skills for explaining the results of analyses and possible risks to senior management and nontechnical audiences.

study for a degree online. If you decide to pursue a degree online, you should check the US Department of Education database of accredited colleges. Accreditation of a college ensures that you can obtain a valid degree and that you can transfer credits to another school, if necessary.

In college, students begin by taking general courses in computer science. Such courses might include Introduction to Computer Systems, programming courses in specific languages, and computational mathematics. In addition, students will take computer science courses in specific areas that interest them. For those interested in working in the energy industry, choices might include robotics, which covers the automating of machines; artificial intelligence and machine learning; data mining; and possibly cybersecurity. Students will most likely take mathematics courses such as advanced forms of calculus and algebra, statistics, and probability, which explain how to analyze the likelihood of various events occurring. Knowledge of engineering and physics principles are important if you are working with software for energy systems. So you will most likely take courses in physics and engineering, as well as experimental design.

If you are interested in developing applications related to the business side of the energy industry, such as financial and risk analysis, taking some courses in finance and economics might be beneficial. For those interested in mining or the oil and gas industries, geology courses help, and for students with an interest in alternative energy, ecology and meteorology courses can aid in understanding how the environment and energy systems interact. Students might also be required to take a course in ethical computing, which covers issues such as how to protect people's privacy and maintain the confidentiality of data.

In addition to technical courses, students will also take humanities and arts courses. Courses in areas such as psychology, the literature and history of other cultures, and foreign languages can be particularly helpful on the job. In the energy industry, you will work with people from diverse cultures and you might have to travel to other countries,

A data analyst shares information on-site with a colleague.

so understanding other people's history and culture will be valuable. Because travel is common in energy jobs, learning a foreign language is desirable as well.

CONTINUING EDUCATION

Getting a job is not the end of a coder's education. New languages, applications, and devices are always being developed. Therefore, programmers in the energy industry have to keep learning new software development techniques, and familiarizing themselves with new hardware technologies. To do so, they might take courses or learn on their own through books, online tutorials, and participation in professional organizations.

The energy industry is evolving and embracing exciting technological advances. Taking STEM courses and developing your skills while in high school is the first step to prepare for further education and embark on a challenging and rewarding career as a programmer in the energy industry.

Glossary

artificial intelligence (AI) The programming of computers to learn and make decisions in a manner similar to the way that human beings do.

big data Vast amount of data captured from databases and direct sources such as sensors.

blackout A complete loss of power in an area.

British thermal unit (Btu) A measure of energy equivalent to the amount of heat needed to raise one pound of water one degree Fahrenheit.

brownout A partial loss of power in an area.

catastrophe A disaster.

chief executive officer (CEO) The head of a company.

cloud The collection of computers housed by service providers at remote locations, on which companies store their data.

cybersecurity The process of protecting computers and data.

data acquisition In terms of computers, the process of collecting data.

data mining Using software to search through very large collections of data to find patterns.

divert To switch from one direction to another.

drone A remotely controlled unmanned vehicle, most often an aircraft.

electronic data interchange (EDI) The exchanging of data between computer systems.

generator A machine that converts mechanical energy from fuel into electricity.

geospatial Relating to a specific location.

greenhouse gas A gas such as carbon dioxide that accumulates in the atmosphere and keeps heat from escaping, contributing to global warming.

hacker A person who breaks into a computer system.

haphazard Random, without a plan.

hydroelectric The conversion of kinetic (motion) energy from running water into electricity.

impedance The amount of resistance an electric component has to the flow of electricity through it.

inhibit To stop.

in-house On a company's premises.

integrate To join together.

internal combustion A process by which gasoline or another fuel is burned to generate energy to power an engine.

internal customer People who work at or have a closer relationship to a company, such as a stakeholder or employee, who also buy materials that the company sells.

load The amount of electricity sent from a power station down a power line.

machine learning (ML) A process by which software is used to allow a computer to improve its responses based on the success of its previous decisions.

mimic To copy.

neural network A computer system that uses connections that mimic those of neurons in the human brain to solve problems.

ozone layer A layer of the gas ozone about 6.2 miles (10 km) above Earth, which absorbs most of the ultraviolet radiation from the sun that reaches Earth, keeping the planet from getting too hot.

portal A point at which customers interact with a company's computer system, such as a website.

predictive Capable of creating forecasts.

predictive maintenance Using computer software to forecast when maintenance on a component is likely to be required.

proliferation Expansion.

query A question posed by a computer using a software language or application.

sensor An electronic device that is placed on a component and sends information on its status to a computer.

substation An assemblage of equipment through which electricity passes and that reduces the high voltage of electrical power to a level suitable for supply to consumers.

synchronize To adjust two or more things so that they occur at the same time.

syntax The rules that govern usage in a human or computer language.

transformer A device that increases or decreases the voltage of electricity that passes through it.

transmission line The line down which electricity is sent from a power station to a home or business.

turbine A machine in which a wheel or rotor, fitted with blades, is made to revolve by a fast-moving stream of water, steam, gas, air, or other fluid, resulting in the generation of electricity.

voice recognition Technology that allows a computer system to interpret human speech.

yield optimization Reducing the amount of fuel used to produce energy when it is likely that demand is going to be low.

Further Information

BOOKS

Allen, John. *Careers in Environmental and Energy Technology.* High-Tech Careers. San Diego, CA: ReferencePoint Press, 2017.

Bedell, Jane. *So You Want to Be a Coder?* New York: Aladdin/ Beyond Words, 2016.

Morgan, Ben, and Steve Setford, eds. *Coding Projects in Python.* New York: Penguin Random House/DK, 2017.

Tweedale, Elizabeth. *How to Code 2.0: Pushing Your Skills Further with Python.* Super Skills. Lake Forest, CA: Walter Foster Jr., 2017.

Xiang, David. *Software Developer Life: Career, Learning, Coding, Daily Life, Stories.* Self-published, Amazon Digital Services, 2018.

WEBSITES
DREAM IN CODE

https://www.dreamincode.net/forums/ forum/78-programming-tutorials
This website provides links to online tutorials for a variety of computer languages for students who want to learn them.

EXXON MOBILE EXPLORE THE OUTLOOK FOR ENERGY: A VIEW TO 2040

https://corporate.exxonmobil.com/en/energy/energy-outlook

Here you can get a detailed look at the new technological developments in the energy industry that are predicted to occur between now and 2040.

GIRL DEVELOP IT

https://www.girldevelopit.com

This website provides information about software development classes and how girls, specifically, can get involved.

ORGANIZATIONS
ASSOCIATION FOR COMPUTING MACHINERY (ACM)

https://www.acm.org

ACM is a major organization for professionals in the computing industry. It offers a variety of resources, including publications specifically for students.

INSTITUTE OF ELECTRICAL AND ELECTRONICS ENGINEERS (IEEE)

https://www.ieee.org

IEEE maintains a student portal on its website for young people interested in technology careers and offers a variety of special programs for them.

Selected Bibliography

Burkhard, Jim, and Tiffany Groode. "The Rivalry Era: A Brief History of the Energy Industry from 2015 to 2040." IHS Markit, October 5, 2014. https://ihsmarkit.com/research-analysis/q14-the-rivalry-era-a-brief-history-of-the-energy-industry-from-2015-to-2040.html.

Colombano, Alfonso, and Ryan Ray. *Careers in the Oil and Gas Industry: A Guidebook of Practical Advice.* Self-published, Amazon CreateSpace, 2018.

"The Development of Energy." ScienceClarified.com. Accessed October 5, 2018. http://www.scienceclarified.com/scitech/Energy-Alternatives/The-Development-of-Energy.html.

"8 Technology Breakthroughs That May Change the Energy Landscape." BP.com. November 26, 2015. https://www.bp.com/en/global/corporate/news-and-insights/bp-magazine/8-technology-breakthroughs-that-may-change-the-energy-landscape.html.

"Energy Data Managers/Statisticians." International Energy Agency. Accessed October 18, 2018. https://www.iea.org/about/jobs/informationonenergydatamanagersstatisticians.

ExxonMobil. *2018 Outlook for Energy: A View to 2040.* Accessed October 17, 2018. https://cdn.exxonmobil.com/~/media/global/files/outlook-for-energy/2018/2018-outlook-for-energy.pdf.

Galvin, Robert, and Kurt Yeager, with Jay Stuller. *Perfect Power: How the Microgrid Revolution Will Unleash Cleaner, Greener, More Abundant Energy.* New York: McGraw Hill, 2009.

Harvey, Abby, Aaron Larson, and Sonal Patel. "History of Power: The Evolution of the Electric Generation Industry." *Power,* October 1, 2017. https://www.powermag.com/history-of-power-the-evolution-of-the-electric-generation-industry.

Hatch, David. "Math, Science, and Computer Students: The Energy Sector Wants You." *US News,* September 10, 2012. https://money.usnews.com/money/careers/articles/2012/09/10/math-science-and-computer-students-the-energy-sector-wants-you.

Kalogirou, Soteris A. "Artificial Intelligence in Renewable Energy Systems Modelling and Prediction." Dept. of Mechanical Engineering, Higher Learning Institute, Cyprus. Accessed October 12, 2018. https://pdfs.semanticscholar.org/03b8/41188867d4fdbaee5ccb056901f506dcf70e.pdf.

KPMG. "Disrupt and Grow." US CEO Outlook 2017. Accessed December 14,2018. https://assets.kpmg.com/content/dam/kpmg/us/pdf/2017/06/us-ceo-outlook-survey-2017.pdf.

Lott, Melissa C. "The Engineer Who Foreshadowed the Smart Grid—in 1921." *Scientific American,* March 30, 2016. https://blogs.scientificamerican.com/plugged-in/the-engineer-who-foreshadowed-the-smart-grid-in-1921.

McNamee, Gregory. *Careers in Renewable Energy: Your World, Your Future*. Masonville, CO: PixyJack Press, 2014.

Mooney, Gavin. "10 Ways Utility Companies Can Use Artificial Intelligence and Machine Learning." *Digitalist Magazine*, May 17, 2018. https://www.digitalistmag.com/digital-economy/2018/05/17/10-ways-utility-companies-can-use-artificial-intelligence-machine-learning-06167501.

"Occupational Outlook Handbook. Software Developers." Bureau of Labor Statistics of the US Department of Labor. Accessed October 23, 2018. https://www.bls.gov/ooh/computer-and-information-technology/software-developers.htm.

Ohri, Anil, and Jyoti Ohri. "Role of Information Technology in Energy Management." *Proceedings of the World Congress on Engineering and Computer Science 2007*, WCECS 2007, October 24-26, 2007, San Francisco, USA.

"Six Next-Generation Technologies That Matter for the Energy Industry." BP.com. Accessed November 5, 2018. https://www.bp.com/en/global/corporate/news-and-insights/bp-magazine/next-generation-technologies-that-matter-for-energy-industry.html.

"Software Engineering Degree: Online and Campus Programs." CollegeGrad.com. Accessed October 20, 2018. https://collegegrad.com/education/computer-technology-and-it/software-engineering.

Index

ABOUT THE AUTHOR

Jeri Freedman has a bachelor of arts degree from Harvard University. For fifteen years she worked for high-technology companies involved in cutting-edge technologies, including advanced semiconductors and scientific testing equipment. She was the cofounder of Innovative Applications, a small computer company selling and customizing accounting software. She is the author of more than fifty young adult nonfiction books, including *Digital Career Building Through Skinning and Modding*, *Careers in Computer Support*, *High-Tech Jobs: Software Development*, and *Cyber Citizenship and Cyber Safety: Intellectual Property*.